After Party

Mary Burritt Christiansen Poetry Series
Hilda Raz, Series Editor

The Mary Burritt Christiansen Poetry Series publishes two to
four books a year that engage and give voice to the realities of
living, working, and experiencing the West and the Border as
places and as metaphors. The purpose of the series is to expand
access to, and the audience for, quality poetry, both single
volumes and anthologies, that can be used for general reading as
well as in classrooms.

Mary Burritt
Christiansen
Poetry Series

Also available in the Mary Burritt Christiansen Poetry Series:

The News as Usual: Poems by Jon Kelly Yenser
Gather the Night: Poems by Katherine DiBella Seluja
The Handyman's Guide to End Times: Poems by Juan J. Morales
Rain Scald: Poems by Tacey M. Atsitty
A Song of Dismantling: Poems by Fernando Pérez
Critical Assembly: Poems of the Manhattan Project by John Canaday
Ground, Wind, This Body: Poems by Tina Carlson
MEAN/TIME: Poems by Grace Bauer
América invertida: An Anthology of Emerging Uruguayan Poets edited by
    Jesse Lee Kercheval
Untrussed: Poems by Christine Stewart-Nuñez

For additional titles in the Mary Burritt Christiansen Poetry Series,
please visit unmpress.com.

AFTER PARTY

Poems

Noah Blaustein

University of New Mexico Press | Albuquerque

Library of Congress Cataloging-in-Publication Data
Names: Blaustein, Noah, 1969– author.
Title: After party: poems / Noah Blaustein.
Description: Albuquerque: University of New Mexico Press, [2019] |
 Series: Mary Burritt Christiansen poetry series |
Identifiers: LCCN 2018034314 (print) | LCCN 2018035258 (e-book) |
 ISBN 9780826360601 (e-book) | ISBN 9780826360595 (pbk.: alk. paper)
Classification: LCC PS3602.L399 (e-book) | LCC PS3602.L399 A6 2019 (print) |
 DDC 811/.6—dc23
LC record available at https://lccn.loc.gov/2018034314

Cover photograph: *Dandelions* by Clark Little
Composed in Dante Mt Std 11.5/13.5

The purpose of poetry is to remind us

how difficult it is to remain just one person,

for our house is open, there are no keys in the doors,

and invisible guests come in and out at will.

—CZESLAW MILOSZ, *Ars Poetica?*

Contents

3.

Moonlight Sonata for the Oughts

I thought you knew me better
than that. Most evenings I prefer
to be an indistinguishable shade
of twilight, generous, but quiet,
present but a thin vapor between
us. 24/7 transcendence was good
enough for the Romantics on paper
but exhausting in practice,
that's why we say *evening*,
this softening of hard edges. I want
to speak flowers to you
but an article on the olinguito
has my attention now, a new
mammal researchers found
in the treetops of the Andes, quietly
munching leaves with their partners
in the fog so the researchers
didn't see them, although they
were looking for 50 years. It's not
that I'm aloof or that I want
to go on living another year
without really moving in
but I bumper-to-bumpered home
& already wolfed down a quickie
dinner. I left a little cronut for you
in the fridge. That pair of mockingbirds
is back at the feeder. I want
to say all this to you, but my voice—
sometimes I think I work at a corporation
built by sorrow. My coworker looked
at me today as if I were thin as a promise
when I asked why we invest
our futures in companies that make
stuff to blow us up. I know
no marriage is fixed like a throat
& we can't just kiss for too long

when we say good-bye but our
vows didn't include lying in bed
with our faces illuminated by rectangles,
our bodies dulling into themselves.
The catkins have neoned the trees
on Sunset Ave. again, that sexless
flowering. I still want you
to find your spot on my chest
tonight, sync your breath to the foghorn—
I'm just not there yet. My life, this
always being singular & plural
at the same time—the Mexican feather
grass wisps orange over the rock garden
but there's no evening here. Just whatever
you're feeling now & me, happy
to be here, on the other side of intimacy.

I

& After

The music still comes from the computer
and the dog still lies in the doorway, one
eyebrow raised to the possibility of squirrels.
I have a sling around my neck
and a baby pressed
against my chest. Her lips are mine,
strangers say, but her nose
is Cristina's. I don't recognize
any of it, the way I type, the tone
in my voice, the giving up of desires
for guessing her desire and the surprise—
I'm happier this way.

Trigger Warning:

Side effects may include digging
a hole in your personal snow

to a time before your heart
floated next to your father's heart

like jars of octopus floating
on a shelf in moonlight

when you watched those hearts
float back to earth

under orange & white parachutes after you
attached model rockets to them

& chased each other around
a field with plastic battle-axes.

California Dreaming

I feel so young.
This backyard, this canyon,
this falling away. The warm
wind out of the desert
has a chill in it. I'm two places
at once. Sage & smog.
I'm holding two sensations
at once and okay with it. I'm
the history of literature. I can't
be alone and I'm always alone—
I had a sugar-coated childhood.
I had rockets in my soup. My two
Davids, where has this middle age
taken you? I was so tired of my little
knowledge on the road I needed
to return to my moon. Yesterday
a mountain lion wandered into
a high-rise lobby. The security guard
paused, waited for the punch line.
He looked at its fur mottled
probably from the rat poisons
pot growers were using to protect
their illegal crops in the national forest
and realized this wasn't a prank
and ran. This is what I know.
Sea miles below. Scrub ticks
in the chaparral. My family
burrito tucked into their blankets
in the house behind me. My family
waking in these mountains
around me. Happiness has always
been a guest in my house that comes
and goes on its own will. It's good
to be close to these stars again.

The Snow Globe of My Youth

            is filled with sand. A green ocean.
Sunset Blvd. lit in eucalyptus
shadow & windshield sun squint
winds through Chumash mesas
& whalebone canyons to septic
beaches. I shake the globe & in
the sand swirl I see that skinhead
chasing me through the Catholic
camp where my Jewish parents
put me and got called into the priest's
office because I refused to say God
in morning prayer. The only God
I believed in was the question mark
& my holy ghost was Jolly Roger,
the dead pirate we were told
shared the cave that formed the right
eye of Skull Rock with a headless bear
& all the children like me who whispered
words like "atheist." I was six. That skinhead.
He videoed himself feeding his twin
brother's rat to his python & left the tape
on his brother's bed. I shake
the snow globe & the swirl shifts
to the after party for a documentary
called *The Parade* in a Chinese bar
without any Chinese. The skinhead has
a limp now & was just on-screen talking
about the night he & some other punks
were listening to speed metal in a debris
basin when a transient walked out
of the scrub brush with a rifle
& started shooting. The skinhead
leans on his cane and is talking
to the ex-Olympian whose blond hair
is a bare lightbulb in this kaleidoscope
of red lanterns. "I don't drink cocktails,"

she says, "only Chardonnay." The skinhead
has written a book. Someone says
your mom is not in it because your mom
was once nice to him. The skinhead
says that before his friends got shot
he was a neo-Nazi but afterward
he grew dreadlocks and played reggae-punk
with the Bad Brains. Shake the globe
again and I'm still in that bar. You can't leave
but you're always trying to leave. The skinhead
keeps getting louder. He is what you were
raised to fear & fight against. He's talking
about the Jetta that went off the cliff & sunk
down to Sunset Reef with a girl you all knew,
her red hair rising to the roof with the engines
last oily bubbles. The skinhead's wife
says that he still suffers from the way
he treated people. "I'll do anything
to make him feel better," she says. A fight
breaks out. Red lanterns are swinging.
The skinhead has someone in a headlock.
I am forty. I am fifteen. I am all sixes.
I've known everyone here most of my life
but they'll always be strangers, the sand
swirl that doesn't settle.

Fable

On this day the Elder Fish told the bear & the girl about the boy who'd gone missing. She said the boy was a good boy & the parents had been arguing about how to punish a good boy for failing to restore their affections to what they once were, honey in their stomachs, Adonis Blue butterflies in their mouths.

The Elder Fish said the searchers searched for a week but found no footprints, no backpack, no prophetic fisherman, no parolee in the great database of deviants & survivors & so the boy's face now yellowed on flyers on poles across the small town.

The Elder Fish said the boy's breath sweeps across the lake in the evenings so the girl whose mouth a stranger once duct-taped & forced to this shore climbed onto that bear who once woke from a brambleberry slumber & chased away a stranger who was standing over a girl like a bear over a fish.

At the mouth of the cave the bear smelled the old smells of deer blood & wild onion, the cigarette butts & yeast perfume of broken Rolling Rocks & used condoms & games of dare & the months of icy dark he once hibernated in but no fresh musk of boy.

The girl rode on that bear's back past where the lodgepole pine trees stop & past where the search-and-rescue dogs had stopped following the scree-squeak hints of rock marmots to a high-altitude tarn where a wolf stood next to a boy's black backpack & blood congealed on the wolf's gray fur.

I will devour you the way you devoured that boy the bear & girl said to the wolf, but as they got closer the wolf grew in size not as all things grow in size when one gets closer but the wolf became bigger than any girl & her bear, bigger than any reflection cast across any long lake.

The girl could see the blood was not a boy's blood but a wound from something much larger than a bullet in an animal much larger than any animal she'd ever seen in a world different from any world she'd known. The wolf's yellow eyes said they'd been shot at for years because they looked like wild.

The wolf said that the boy was here that other children were here that they come here years before their parents their mothers their fathers with their coat-hanger switches & hot irons ever notice them wander off into themselves into this scree meadow where all those stupid you-fucked-up-my-life sentences don't reach them.

Look,
    the yellow eyes of the wolf said,
                tiger lily,
                    falling aster.

Coming-of-Age Story # ∞: Angry Bastard Theory

A look exchanged and then blows.
That look and then a heartbeat
decision:

       haymaker him
before he can shake the bees
from between his ears

or kick him in his stomach
as he gets up to all fours,
finish him the way man-boys do?

Leg as pestle, pavement as mortar.
His face-head-hair a little nutmeg seed
to grind and sprinkle on my hot youth.

"Peace man," Barry, who wears
a skanking ska-man army jacket, says.
"It's over. Peeeeeeeeace!"

Friends with what-the-fuck faces
wonder how it happened
because I'm not a what-the-fuck kid.

"Dude," Ghodes says, "look
at your hand." Blood.
And bone?

Those flesh-pink stucco bungalows
float on the blacktop in the distance—
the color of postwar 1950s happy.

I've got class to get to.
Keon grabs my shoulder, spins
me into a cheap shot,

into his fist mushing
my lip into my braces.
"Stop," I say.

"We're friends."
And the next day
he shows me his new

silver-and-pearl-handled
semiautomatic.
We laugh.

———

My daughter stops my reading
to ask if I've ever been
in trouble. Today she received
a green star for good behavior
and stuck it to her bunk bed.
I clasp my hands to hide
what she won't notice,
how my right pinkie, when pressed
against the left, is a half-inch shorter,
my knuckle floats somewhere
near my wrist. "Boxer's fracture,"
the principal read from the doctor's
report aloud to my dad and me
and Keon. (His parents were never
around.) I didn't tell my daughter
that the dad I introduced her to
at ice cream once said something
about me being a Jew
for not sharing my bagel and so I said
something back about kung fu

because he's part Korean (always r&r,
race and religion) and that in the water
today he paddled up to me, thirty years
after I broke that bone on his temple,
and said, "It really is over now. I do
know kung fu! I got my purple belt."
I didn't say that sometimes I still
wonder what his skull would've felt
like crushing under the weight of my
confusion but that most of the time
I shake my head because I don't know
why I swung or why I stopped. "I think
it's time," I tell her, "you close your eyes,
and listen to me read this story:
'Once there was a little bunny
who wanted to run away.'"

After Party

The Hello Kitty piñata's head
swings from the pepper tree—
a sweet decapitation. Glitter
across the rental table & pink
paper flowers wilt in the succulents.
This is the stale beer & cigarettes
of 7-year-olds. "My fluffy puppy
is so soft" still means "my fluffy
puppy is so soft." I'm seducing
my wife the way good men
of my generation do, by rinsing
blue & red sticky plates, taking out
heavy cake-trash. I'm celebrating
their lack of cool. No fights
over girls or boys to save face,
just little leopard faces everywhere.

El Niño, El Viejo, El Viento

He left Wednesday to wander the Southwest.
I arrived yesterday as the red walkway began to cool.
I keep expecting the park service to call, tell me
they've found a man in deMaria's Field with a net

waiting for nightfall to catch lightning.
They'll tell me he mutters for a Paula,
for a lost wife, and asks if we know
Degas copied Rembrandt's light.

The morning glory sags the deck
railing under its amassed weight,
bends the electrical piping
into purple flowers of neglect.

The day's shadows have already stood up straight
and now begin to lean as if wanting to rest.
A pound or, roughly, one thousand
five hundred screws. Ten gallons of deck stain.

My plan: stain surfaces with linseed,
hammer memory into a place, and then,
when he returns, apologize
and suggest he sell.

He'll say, "I'd rather flake away
with the paint on my brushes,
rot with my depreciating decks,
than move into the smog.

I've had second and third lives since she passed,
since you, your brother, moved on—
I've been fortunate."
And he has.

The Santa Anas gather screws into the cracks
and with a nail I split open a wasp house
creviced between the 2x4s and the eggs,
those little bits of xerophytic sap, are dried.

Hip & Now

Those years black wasps hummed
under my skin & every word stung.

I wrote manifestos in invisible ink
& thought myself a revolutionary.

Our first holiday lights faded through half-lidded windows.
No balsa airplanes loopy looped the airspace over our deck.

We taught ourselves sign language
so I'd learn to speak with greater care.

A family of crows kept bringing night in on their backs—
that year, that sky, red to black, red to black

& then a black calendar with silver moons & red
hearts dangled from the fridge, daringly.

"The rate of successful conception past the age of 36
decreases exponentially year over year," you said.

The sun corrugates my shed roof now.
Steam rises from my tea.

You're at work, probably asleep, lullabied
by the hum of the ER's V-tach rhythms.

I didn't fret over the world's violences last night
& neither one of our kids cried out—

I no longer apologize for this:
my office smells like bergamot.

Prince Lightning, Prince Thunder

That shelf dedicated to the titles
of your life, the work and joy of it,
flashes clear. Airplanes must have
seeded the clouds through the night
to grow rain. I've almost slept until dawn
without shame. The beautiful
younger poet whose smile and lines
you can't shake—not your first
thought. I'm waiting for thunder.
I'm waiting for lightning to see
if the light passes through me
where my heart and lungs should be
or if I will blink at my hand tossing
blueberries & raspberries into a bath
of oatmeal & soy milk. I fell asleep
reading an obituary & weather science
at the same time, death & shifts
in atmospheric pressure. The pop icon's
death was due to a hole in his heart. His
death was due to an overdose. His death
is unknown & unknowable and the silver
iodide the good people from Public Works
fired from secret cannons to make
the drought evaporate may be saving us
from dehydration or they may be putting
microscopic holes through you and me. If
there's thunder, I'm going to last a little
longer before I lose my cool following
my son from room to room to make sure
all the curious books of this house
& all the curious things of this world
don't keep him from finding his neon
yellow sweatshirt among the piles
of my bachelor-black boxers. "I'm on
the downslope of my forties" I can hear
a drug dealer I used to hang out with

say. "Don't wait for thunder" I can hear
my old therapist say. "Be like water.
Water has no scars." "What's it like
to be the best guitarist in the world?"
a journalist asked Clapton. "I don't know,"
he said, "go ask Prince." That Prince
of the obituary that made my eyes go heavy
last night & that Prince whose Purple Rain
funked up my dreams. For fifteen years
I partied overtime, waited for thunder,
waited for the party of a century
that's now fifteen years past. Every day
the free radicals of my youth pass
from us & the youth take up their old ideas
as if they were their own & revolutionary.
There are many tiny holes in my heart
from all the people I am secretly in love with
which means I still want to be satisfied
& never satisfied. In the next two minutes
a friend will text me an invite to another
prince's funeral, Prince Buster, the original
prince of "Madness" & my ex-wife
will text to let me know she bought a Tesla
& not to freak out at pick-up & my new
something-or-other will ask if I want
to get a cabin this weekend to watch clouds
& read Dante in bed. If there was thunder.
If there was lightning. I did not notice. "Ok,
whatever you want" I text my ex back. I was
fun to be married to but I was never great
at being responsible. When I fill out
the tardy slip the principal gives me
a private smile. I once surfed Mavericks
with Ingrid, the woman she ditched
her husband for. I write the facts:
"We're late because the giant squid
has three brains & its DNA is not
believed to be from this world."

2

Coming-of-Age Story: Icons

A blue moon this dawn and I'm
thinking of Buson—
          "Field of bright mustard,
the moon in the east,
          the sun in the west"—
and James Bond, the dusty theater
in which honeyed sex dripped down
the naked shadows through the opening
credits on screen. I thought
that *A Man with a Golden Gun*
was what a "real" man was supposed to be
& the world was full of seven-foot-tall
men with steel teeth named Jaws
who wanted to be loved so bad
they would help destroy the world
by killing me. My single-digit
life had already been shaken
& I wanted to float in a space
capsule on a transparent ocean
while someone called to see if I was safe,
if the spy who loved me was safe. My
father was doing his best to teach
me the reasons for the spots on a tiger
lily but I'd already seen what dressing
in a suit and tie to look like and to please
other men for twelve hours a day
does to the spine
& so I was looking for something more
than one week off a year to float
pumice stones on high-altitude tarns.
51 weeks of the year for 35 years
my father left at seven and came home
exhausted at seven without ever getting sick
but never loved the men he worked for
which I knew even then was a type of sickness.
I practiced my British accent in secret
& wanted to become more straight-haired

less Jewfro more debonair & laissez-faire not
everything has to be a political debate. In that
dark theater real men spoke with accents,
wore tuxedos & had secret weapon pens
they could save the sun from the cold war,
from men with fall-away floors over aquariums
full of sharks. Real men didn't send
their kids to school in the hood
to support equality & get into
brouhahas for hiring men & women
not like them. That week my father
did what he thought a man should do
with a kid, teach them to identify
pine trees by the number of needles
in a bunch, compliment me for running
fast like the Olympian on the cereal box
that is now a woman—"You don't
just leave the door open for Ishmael,"
he would say. Spy morning moon
through vapor-thin curtains—
I woke in that chipmunk-holed
hippie cabin & listened to my father
ready to disappear into the Sierras
& return with breakfast. When I heard
no deck rustle, no wind shift
through vanilla pine, I imagined
my mummy bag was a silk cocoon
& I was rapt by a Russian-accented
dark-haired green-eyed gorgeous
who helped me save *Moonraker*
& was trying not to let her champagne giggles
bubble over into the CB as we floated
in our space capsule after reentry in some
tropical ocean & a voice called out:
"Double-O-Seven. Are you there?
Come in. Double-O . . .?"

What's Going On?

"You've got to give a little to get a little,"
the car salesman says on the phone
like I'm back in C. Anderson's Sirocco
& it's the '80s & he's telling me to give
a little cash for shooters for the girls
coming over b/c you've got to give
a little, etc. The pool's reflection
shimmers on my dad's bedroom ceiling
& makes Danielle S. & me feel bubbly
as she lies across the Cal King & asks
for another beer & I drop trou & say,
"You've got to give a little if you want
to get a little," the way C. Anderson told me
to & her eyes go blackberry big b/c she
doesn't know what to do & my eyes
go blackberry large b/c I'm pretending
that I do. We both don't know
what to say b/c we've been told
this will be wonderful but we don't
feel wonderful. My yellow Gotcha surf
shorts are damp around my tanned ankles
just like a spread I saw in a neighbor's *Oui*—
Give a little. Get a little. Let me think
about it I hear my voice say to the salesman
which is what straight-brown-hair-
to-her-lower-back Danielle S. should've said
& hang up & go outside to see what's
going on. "The sound from a helicopter's
blades is just displaced air, like a breath,"
my son said the other night, proud
of his new knowledge and my neighbor
says, "Haven't you heard? There was a shooter
walking up Pico Blvd. & the president
was passing through & is okay but the schools
are on lockdown & no one knows anything

about our kids." On the TV men
& women with bulletproof vests
over their neckties are saying give us
a little more time & a teen man-boy lies
facedown in a black flak jacket of blood
in front of the juco library & they're trying
to figure out if he was the only shooter
& if he was the only one to set fire
to the two houses on 29th & shoot
at buses & elementary schools & passersby
for ten blocks past the cemetery
all the way down to the campus. "Sequester
in place," a helicopter says, which sounds
like "Sequester in *peace*." *Sequester*, a transitive
verb, to hold until a debt's been repaid. What
body, what mind is not transitive? A woman
I've seen in the smoothie bar is wearing body
armor over her yoga stretch-pants & top
& the initials of a government agency
I was raised to be wary of are printed on her back
& she's kneeling with an assault rifle
& a reporter is wondering what did
this shooter—never a girl—give
to become this morning's impotent king
of all transitive verbs? What deluded debt
did the janitor's body & his daughter's
body repay & what debt would my boy's
body repay? A kid my kindergartner's age
with a lip split looks at me from the mailer
on my desk from the place that sends doctors
to fix kids' lips in parts of the world
I've mostly never been & asks that I give
again & change a life & that I have choices
to whom & to what I give. Muzak plays
"Give Me All Your Love" without irony

in some hallway command center as another
jowly community-relations officer says,
"The situation is stabilizing but still fluid.
Please be patient; give us more time." Give
us all more time. Give us all back
what we hope hasn't been taken,
I say aloud to no god in particular.

Tide Pool

The old oceans return us, slowly tug us,
along the familiar fiction of childhood.
—NORMAN DUBIE, "Popham of the New Song"

I'm dating my 16-year-old
self again. I'm a romantic dog. Woody
Allen is a hero & Portnoy a god
but I've yet to rub Buddha's fat
vegan belly. In my free time
I still think my time is free. I ditch
my public education staring at the holes
in the asbestos ceiling tile & read
Plato at Jetty because I've been told
he was serious & I want to be serious
even though I can't stop punctuating
every sentence with "dude." Most
Californian sea life is dull-brown or gray
except for sea anemone, which are blue
or red. The jetty smells of sea lions
& fishermen but I've never seen
a sea lion or fishermen there, only
a baby great white once after a storm,
jaw opened on the wet rock, too small
to fit around my knee, its incisors
kind of cute. My life's already been
punctuated by death & ecstasy,
cranial needles & feral dogs
chasing us mezcal-eyed on horseback
through Ensenada's *barrio muerte*
so I think that qualifies me to be a poet
even though I'm not really sure
what a poet does. "But," Katie says,
"you can't be special in this city

unless you're a movie star & why
would you want to do *that*?" I've
shown her my spot on the rocks
at Sunset & PCH & shown her
my wave doodles in the foreword
of Plato because I can't focus
long enough to make it through
the first page. "Look," I say & poke
the mouth of a red anemone
so it wraps its sticky around
my poke & shudders as though
it were midnight & my finger
was a grunion come ashore to mate
& I am now a piece of moonlight
caught flopping back to join the rest
of the ocean's moonlight. Katie
is from a family that uses words
like "proper"—her parents say
I got an artist for a dad. Red
crabs shadow in the rocks
& move their turret eyes
every time we touch hands.
"You're so obvious," she says.

Toast

Alison Dent was teasing. That li'l Ms. Dent, whose
father was a dentist, no joke, & whose sister
was already famous for her blowies. My weekend
news had gone jr. high–viral. I'd got caught

in a thicket, Wendy Katz showing me
her kindness, soothing me through
my mother's wake, the toasts, my real
bar mitzvah. Alison was saying on the bus

that last year I was too shy to touch her hand,
that I would've never marveled, openly,
about the Fonz, what kind of skateboard
it takes to snap your fingers & make a girl swoon.

The bus doors vacuumed shut & Alison's sweet
voice swirled into the plumes of black diesel,
into Sunset's hollow-traffic whoosh, into that
walk past those Ms. Lonelyhearts Apartments.

To that house. That driveway, that mouth
of Little Las Pulgas Canyon, little flea canyon,
that white stucco, that textured siding that
collects all of southern California's sadnesses.

That taste of my mother's wine
in my CPR mouth,
                vinegar still.
That CEO, my father's boss,

calling to offer to send him
a whore for his sorrows
while my ghost sister baked
heroin bread in my mom's Magic Chef.

I did what my mom would've done:
I brown-sugared & cinnamoned
a piece of bread. I watched the new
toaster oven amber, that body of bread darken.

How long does it take for a parent's
body to go to ash? There was algebra
to do. There was the striped skull
of a black-crowned sparrow in the bamboo.

Buttery-sweet-cinnamon-sugar bubbles
rose in the center of the toast
& popped in the still air.
This was *was*.

Topanga Beach, West Lot

"A little boost so you
      won't feel the water,
those pink fingers going blue."

Witheral's Tahitian orphan moon face
      leaning out his new black 4Runner
offering bumps & gummies.

Cut with his own credit card
      coke lines on a hand mirror
look like swell filling in.

—

Her leopard-print bikini in a carport
      crash pad. Her whispers in my ear
as the Dream Syndicate guitar riffs in the background.

I didn't know what to do with stillness yet,
      when the ocean went flat
& the rhythms in my head

wouldn't let me into the books
      I'd learn to love. "Just a few dollars," she was whispering,
"and I'll take you all the way home."

—

My father, Yom Kippured by walking in the soft sand.
      That afternoon I broke his silences by asking,
"That beach up there with the pine tree, is that Hawaii?"

His blue-eyed glare hushed me. Neil Young & Manson
        squatted in the condemned shoreline shacks
with the surfers who guarded that need-a-fix light

with shotguns. "Once you fall in love
        with a form," my father said,
"you'll die before you let it go."

———

Her firebird on that sand-colored Camaro
        plumes my memory
in a gas cloud & erases names.

How far would I go to drop life's quadratic equations
        for the way cocoa butter & salt
blister the air?

We called each other Homes
        because we had none.
What up, Homes?

———

Chaca gives us Quiksilver trunks
        from his trunk to hook us
up 'cause "we're bros."

In the half-gram light of dawn
        he backed his Sirocco through the surf
shop window & filled his trunk with kit

clothes & skegs & piña-colada wax & citrus resin—
      I learned to look out for ghosts
because they always do what causes the most pain.

Remembering the Decade

The first fish with sun cancer.
The first thousand fish.

Bamboo against slate in sun.
Bamboo against slate in rain.

The weather report:
drips from your air conditioner will be increasing.

A storm cloud hovered over the Council for Catastrophic Science.
The debate—do tsunamis move like Ferris wheels?—
was ended by a tsunami.

Catastrophic earthquake, terrorists, tidal surge, firestorm, West Nile
    virus,
bird flu, swine flu, storm of the century, mass murder, mega terrorist,

mega-mega terrorist, mega-mega deal, mega-mega storm,
    mega-mega earthquake.
Your mega may be bigger than my mega but my mega-mega will beat
your mega big any day.

A lot of Old Testament. But no fun stuff?
Talking snakes? The giant ship? The parting ocean?

"Naturally occurring phenomena." "The new normal." "Naturally
    occurring phenomena."
"The new normal." "Naturally occurring phenomena." "The new
    normal."

Those Koch brothers high on their own coal dust.
"Food shortages, human devastation, are just engineering problems."

Here's a solution: shoot a two-thousand-square-foot piece of glass
with a magnetic gun into space to reflect two percent of the sun.

It's over a hundred on the deck. Toby, the dog,
is sitting in the pollution-cooled spring.
I think I'm going to join him.

The first fish with sun cancer.
The first thousand fish.

Bamboo against slate in sun.
Bamboo against slate in rain.

Tattoo: Poses 2 & 5

What men can't own they try to stain—
I know—but his hand is the sun that moves
the Plumeria my ex inked onto my right hip.
He's my samurai. He might be the one
who can tame the dragon snake
that wraps around the black flower
between my shoulder blades. My jellyfish
heart—it's almost quivering with hope again
but why does he want to flip me over,
bukake the purple shunga wave
that washes over my lower back, white
out that ex's signature, gesso me
as if I could be a blank canvas again?
"I'm cool with the others who've come
before me," he said but the way he's rubbing
himself into me—does he think
he can take away the slumber commitment
brings? Take away that Mr. Buttermilk
fiancé I left in the burbs to raise my body
into skin art's ecstasies? He'll find out
like they all find out, my fuckups
are etched into my pleasures.

Fracture & Want

Here, the sand on the pavement,
a type of carpet. The where I go
to turn on my quiet. Then, the where
I went to blow things up. In front
of an ocean you're always a slow
fade. Then, the need to wake Wild
Turkey breathed. Here, no owl,
no whiskey who who? The reds
burn into heliotropes & I become
black silhouette, indistinguishable
from pavement. That decade
returning to that shade & scree
canyon. That bay-laurel canyon
& my father's nude models
placing their thumbprints on my
cerebellum. & want. His adult
students come for something
more from this life, from him,
& that earnest scrub-oak light
& earnest nipple shadowing out
of her paisley cotton throw light.
I would say something to sound
cool, maybe about Ernst or Schiele—
sycophantic bullshit—and invite
them over later for some "scotch
& tofu." Here, the quiet I collect.
This evening. Then, I was the slow
fade. Fracture. Those interiors
of LA's always-darkened bars. That
Botticelli model underneath me, the last
of his models. The orange streetlight
through her thin curtains,
that relentless light collecting
on the sweat between her breasts,
"Fuck me from behind," she said,
"so you can finish & leave. I'm
over your ekphrastic bullshit."

Tattoo Nude: Fan Mail, Pose #4 (More Ars Poetica)

This photo you've sent to me, a near stranger—my morning coffee. A way to enter into you. A close up. The tattooed curve of the orange carp's head mimics the curve of your ass. The wall behind, the bedspread you lie on, your skin, all the same color, a type of soft-focus canvas. The photo is off-center, so the carp is on the lower left, your crack & hidden folds of labia on the right. The viewer is pulled between the two dark parts of the photo—the carp's eye or the eye we can't see. The photographer has asked us to choose & so you've asked me to choose. The carp's eye is fierce & full of terror, running away from something at the same time its eyelid, its eyelash, beckons.

Lemons

That reserved patois of adult men:
"Which one is yours?
What do you do . . .?"

The skate instructor is dressed
as a dragon & twirling
in disco ball light.

"I'm a lawyer."
"I'm Steve Pro," he said—
"Holy shit," I said.

Doughy pizza & doughy birthday cake
on a table & blue thank-you bags
slouched in a dank corner.

"You're the one
that blinded me
when I was ten," I said.

Someone walked in
from the sun outside
& broke the rink's black light.

"Oh my god," he said.
"Do you think
I can still sue?" I said.

It was funny.
But he didn't laugh.
It'd been thirty years.

—

Halloween.

That shaving cream that smelled
like gasoline & smoked mash,
what men were supposed to smell like
which made us happy to still be boys.

We went out to trick houses
that didn't treat, that door
opening too late. A man
yelling
his wife was bedridden
as we ran. *Fuckers.*

Then the older boys saw us. Steve's crew
of crash victims & dead presidents,
against us, pirates & superheroes. My
shaving-cream shooter coated
the peach fuzz of a green vampire.

I was laughing. Everyone was laughing.
Then my candy bag pillowed
my head. High-pitched
hiss hum. The smell & sting
of lemons, of blood & gasoline,
of citric acid cauterizing my eye.

Someone had thrown an unripe
lemon, just right.

—

Your baby. The pulp in his eye
& brow. "You'll be fine," you comfort
him as he throws up from the ocular
fracture. It's just a concussion. Show
concern but not worry. Tell him to be

still. To rest. You said, "Be careful"
when he went out with a can of shaving
cream & a bag for candy & came
home with shut-swollen-purple-
right-side-of-face eye—it happens.
Give him a rib eye. An eye
for an I. Remember the secret
to parenting. Show concern,
but not worry, even when you
don't know how bad something
is about to go. You've hid your own
radioactive aches for years so this
should be easy. Iced red meat
on purple flesh. You'll be fine.

—

Another ocular pressure test
in another specialist's office, my
forehead pressed into a plastic
forehead cup. My chin pressed
into another chin cup. Three
floors below, the handlebar-
mustached man who cuts my hair
smokes a cigarette & says hello
to someone in a muscle car
playing "What's Going On."
"Look at the red light" I am
told. Pretend it is a train
light in a tunnel. Don't jump
away. "Don't be afraid" is what
parents say when they need you
to do something that has great
potential to suck. Children with sick
parents learn to compete through
suffering & what I wanted in that

world of model rockets & respirators
was to be heard. An air mass
when shot out of an optical cannon
looks like a dust storm before it hits
your eye, before it tells you
if you'll see again. Every living
thing in this world has some
pressure. Keep your chin in
the black cup. Look at that red
light in total darkness. It is a plane
in the sky. A boat at sea. "Don't
move your head." A little rocket ship . . .

—

Dear Mr. Pro,

I've never had a language
to speak with my brother
about things that matter

so if you happen to read this
would you please tell me
what's true? I heard

my brother
caught you
at a party that night

& his friends held down
your arms & legs
while he held a fire extinguisher

to your face
did right by me
foamed your mouth

until green bubbles
foamed from your nose
& you got some crazy strength

& threw them off.
Once I asked my brother
did he press that black

nozzle into your blue eyes
for me & he said, "you don't
know what you're talking about."

I'm not religious enough
to believe in retribution,
your eye in exchange for mine,

but that idea of my brother
made the world
a little less big.

What did your lawyer
father say to my father
to back him down?

What did he have on us
better than a white curb
with a bloodied lemon?

—

The man who, as a teen, threw a lemon
that took a boy's eyesight from one eye
said that as a teen his parents
never let him forget &
that he still struggles
with a more violent image of himself

than others see in him
so I said that I was lucky
the doctors said nerve endings
don't regenerate but mine did
so now there's a little scarring
but you're looking into an eye
famous with certain specialists
that my parents loved me
& I loved them back
that my father understood
I'd have no depth perception
that I wouldn't be able
to discern special relationships
& so my father made a Ping-Pong table
& we played every night
until I could see again.

—

The city I live in is famous
for its farmer's market
& self-defense classes
they teach to 3-year-olds.

My son can't read yet
but he can spin kick.
In the black shadow of a high-rise
shoppers pick over lemons.

They look like small lanterns
& the shoppers are warming
their hands. My son, in his *gi*,
asks how you make lemonade.
The lemon came over with Columbus,
most likely from India,

the word itself
probably Middle Eastern.

The one that took my sight
was most likely a Eureka,
although a Meyer, the Typhoid Mary
of lemons, is a distinct possibility.

"Water, and sugar, and lemon juice,"
I say to my son. Anything can be a weapon
but there's no defense for a lemon
in your hand, that bright weight.

3

Temple

The speed of the humdrum
we return to. My son taps
out a syncopation with his
fork. The hair dryer &
my wife's voice, "August,
put on your shoes." There
are forms to fill out. Practices
to get to. Practice: I close
my eyes. In Japan my kids
couldn't wait to replace
the rock of the train & humidity
of the temples with the salve
of the hotel pool. Was it Issa
I chanted as I passed the Orange
Fürer on the news in the bar,
"In Kyoto / the bureaucrat speaks /
the cuckoo sings"? That hotel pool
separated by a massive glass wall
at the base of a stagger-stepped
waterfall so that water rushed
toward you but stopped at the glass
like the ways in which the city
stopped at the walls of its shrines.
The waterfall, the pool shimmered
on the ceiling, grotto-like & we floated
& looked out at the water rushing toward us
& closed our eyes & tried to still the rush
of the rush-hour trains, of travel,
of the Shinto sign for shrine
I had trouble separating
from a swastika even though
the symbol, the lines, as Garret said,
go the other way, both literally
& figuratively. Once the symbol
of evil is burned into your eyelids
it's difficult to reverse its impression.

That wet heat that pulse of tourists
pressed against our skin as we paused
to look at Rokuon-Ji, the golden temple
floating on that green lake. I floated
& tried to hold the image of the gold
temple in my head & not the story
of the monk with a persecution complex
who burned it down in the '50s. Gold,
the color of reflection. Gold, the color
to ward off boredom
                   & thoughts of death.

Androids Don't Just Dream of Electric Sheep

For Phillip K. Dick

She likes the way I orbit around my blue
energy cube. Everything in this outer
galaxy is very real when you let yourself
forget it is not. The way they make Clear
Fall™ here & Virtual Surf™ lulls me into belief
but thoughts of Ashly still creep in.
I selected Marine Layer Melancholy™
as my weather of choice this evening
& ordered the droid with the silk
arms to sit in front of the Faux Fire™
with. I'm still kind of sort of faithful
to Ashly even though I don't know
if she made it to a different moon
& my telepathies no longer get
through. In this atmosphere I've gone
53 minutes without thinking about
how that president let those gasses
surround our houses, how the sky
went sunsmoke, that last bomb
lowering the sky, the sky & you, Ashly,
going out through that hole in that sky.
"You just can't fill my loneliness," a woman
said to her husband in the last
century. I woke myself up this morning
with a healthy dose of Focus™, the drug,
this morning so none of the smoke
in my bones from our old orbits would seep
into my blood. "Put down that book"
Claudia Bot™ says. "This is our party &
I'm programmed to not let you be lonely."

What Happens Next I Will Think About Later

My shoulders raise & my head lowers—
a loud boom, an explosion as I walk
away from my old minivan, my old life,
in the new-car lot. "Fireworks?" I ask
the salesman. He's saying something
about the latest ways to stay connected
to my loved ones in a new car, even
as I drive myself farther away. "You'll
never need to be alone again," he says
with a straight face that makes my back
tighten. Most of the people I meet have
made their money buying or selling
things they don't care much about
made by people they'll never know
but the people I tend to love
love making beautiful things & give
them away almost for free. My old
professor called his wagon Sir Lancelot
& drove it until his foot went through
the floor and he looked at his storekeeper
buddy in the passenger seat & they looked
down at the chunks of sooty-ice crud
on the asphalt passing under their feet
& started laughing & canceled the lecture
& went to the nearest dealership. "What
does new satisfy?" every married man
& woman in their forties should ask
themselves each morning before they walk
out the door. Ba-Boom! Another explosion.
"For New Year's Eve?" I ask. "No," Phil
the sales guy says. "They store the strawberries
from the fields around us on the other side,"
he says, pointing to a cinder-block wall
towering over the fields & cars at the far
end of the lot, a miniature Great Wall,
an impromptu giant screen for the sunset

to project its death-heart colors. That story:
the pickers in the fields needing to believe
in a heaven. This story: the shoppers
in the car lots needing faith to dig themselves
another debt grave. "They've got a guy,"
the salesman says motioning to the wall,
"whose job it is to do nothing but throw
explosives at the birds trying to eat
the berries all day. When the picking
gets heavy, he'll even light entire propane
tanks on fire. Those really make you
jump out of your stomach." A son pulls
his father's hand away from the sales
sticker on a Swagger Wagon. "Ninjas
never poop their pants," the father says
to his boy. Where is the god of the stomach
bug? Where is the god that makes ravens
peck at all the shiny in this world? El Niño's
baby chill is creeping up my leg. "How 'bout
the 4x4?" the salesman directs. "This winter's
going to be a rough one." Boom. The sky's
full of red seagulls. I am a raven.
I've never known an honest god.

"That's God's Work"

1.

That's what Chris said but I was thinking
more about that poem I read in college
because it had "pissing" in the title
because I wanted to know how "good poets"
turn pissing off of the back of a boat
into something worth reading
and I remember being amazed
by how he turned his uric-acid dribble
into a metaphor for a long sentence
and a treatise on how language
was the one thing stolen from the gods
that could keep changing and still be beautiful
no matter the century but I was critical
of the poem too because the turning of piss
into metaphor seemed like an intellectual flinch
or an apology for writing about the body at all
when it seemed to me that any moment
could be made "poetic" on its own
without dragging gods and theory into it.

2.

I'd just finished telling Chris
about Kathleen's last 24-hr. shift
how she was asleep in her call room
having a working mother's anxiety dream
her daughter's voice calling to her
from the pantry from an empty pasta pot
when the hospital alarm went off
and the floor nurse called to say, "Room four's coded"
and so from the world of guilty dreams
to florescent lights and blue alarm lights
reflecting on the sterile floors
in the halls and stairwell she blinked and ran
the intercom repeating "code blue"

90 seconds to get into the O.R. and baby out of mom
to get mom's heart beating & stabilized
one minute and 10 seconds when the doctor
and her assist ran through opposite doors
gowns and gloves and face masks ready to go
Kathleen still blinking from sleep
from thoughts of the ex she bumped into
at the stoplight in his truck his name
& contractor's license on the door in blue
on her way in this morning
the last time she saw him he hit her
& she called the cops changed the locks
& took out a restraining order & all that
shoved somewhere deep back into the oblongata
the patient prepped her belly her pubis
shaved and splattered with Betadine before her
almost faceless everyone masked and almost faceless
the patient the top half of her body curtained off
60 seconds to go   both doctors reaching for scalpels
after 1,000 times anything can become old hat
& then pausing seconds to read the patient's tattoo
stretched out from pelvis bone to pelvis bone
the letters made even more bold by the pregnancy
EAT ME RIGHT OR GET OUT OF SIGHT
and so eyes met and so Kathleen asked,
"Here or here?" moving the scalpel
questioning whether or not to split
the "OR" with a scar or leave
the unstressed syllable intact
green lettering on honeydew skin
45 seconds to go
but they took their time sewing her up
joking whether or not to move around
a letter or two and agreeing that what she really needed
what both doctors really needed
was to add a "Tr" before the "eat"
and then debated whether or not
it was a three-beat line that should

be broken after the unstressed syllable—
a poet had recently visited their hospital—
or a six-beat line that should be left intact
and quietly imagined to themselves
what she might say to her new daughter
in six years when she begins to read.

There Is No Thou to Speak of

A 17-year-old balances
on the parking block while the police
say, "Count backward." That 17-year-old
now pays a mortgage & his children hear
an echo when they call his name. They want
him to make them dinner but he's
fourteen again and being chased
from a surf spot in Baja by wild dogs
& now a youngish man appears
on his screen with impossible abs
and smooth boxer briefs. He needs
underwear. This weekend is supposed
to be hot. The summer pool
will be open for one day. They have
swim lessons. His kids need to learn
to swim. His wife calls his name. He's
drinking 25-year-old Old Blowhard with a 24-
year-old Southern belle in an Atlanta hotel.
He's deleting photos of himself wearing
red panties as a bandanna from the Cloud.
There was a canopy bed. There was a porch.
A sugar magnolia. "'Round Midnight"
on the stereo. This isn't guilt. He needed
his girl. He needed. He was a boy
trying to remember his name. He's a boy
who is a man who is a boy who's
figuring out how to be a man
that drives a minivan. An ocean, a green
wave peels across his screen. A stock
is skyrocketing today. Another stock
is plummeting. What to do next?
Thou? Where art?

This Year. Last Year.

The boy down the street tosses
the ball through the garage hoop
& Mr. Lincoln, the neighbor's cat,
keeps scratching at the compost heap
for eggshells but there's that smell
of something sweet & smoky in the air,
memory wafting across the lawns.
This year, no more waiting for
the angelic clouds in the city of angels
to appear or an ex-boss to call & offer
to keep me from drifting, to keep
me from regressing into that man-boy
outside Bob's market asking women
to buy him beer or give him
a kiss. Suffering is measured
by the strength of one's fears. The way
I used to close my eyes & show up outside
my neighbor's bedroom in the smiley-
face boxers my wife gave me. Worse,
what happened when she let me in. Even
with that smell afloat, the blue frog
on the red Sugar Smacks™ box
doesn't stop grinning from on top
of the neighbor's fridge into my window
the same as it has since we moved in.
Anxiety is broken by the details
one notices. Your neighbor goes
to work at 7:45 & returns at 6:15

with a stripe of sweat down the center
of her jogging bra. Thus marks the end
of a year & the beginning of a year
of night suns in the park blazing
each evening & the kids continuing
to show up & wait for an adult
to yell, "Kick the ball!" & a parent
to say afterward, "Good job!" This
year will not be like last year—my heart,
a hummingbird heart. No black moths
will beat against my rib cage. Just kids
showing up in uniforms like yellow
jackets. Just the sweet of evening
through my window like rose hip tea.

I'm on a Good Mixture & I Don't Want to Waste It

I've taken a go pill to keep
the brown widow that dangled
its red hourglass in front of my door
from crawling into my day. A get-
me-through-it pill in place of coffee's
catapult ride. A capsule-raft to float
through the river of papers
on my desk. An I-don't-want-to-lose-
my-shit-today pill in the latest
rash of selfies of people smiling
next to their cars stopped on the 805
as a man teeters on the overpass
in the background. "There's no
deep feeling left in the world,"
the man yelled to the crisis
negotiator, "only keystroke
knowledge of things." An I'm-not-
going-to-teeter pill, at least not
today. The green-blue of a hummingbird's
back disappears into the green-blue
leaves of a eucalyptus grove. I've taken
a no-more-hummingbird-brain
pill. In college people used to love
to say Kerouac wrote *On the Road*
in 24 hrs. on speed but now speed
is just another bomb prescribed
to induce calm in the hyperactive.
How do you learn this trick of absorbing
a story without the story changing
your day? My son's plastic cup

bounces off the floor but keeps
its shape. I've taken a plastic-
cup pill. But here's a story about a Russian
knifing his best friend b/c his friend
said poetry's nothing but pretty
images & distraction. Try to pick
your distractions your ex used to say.
Dawn sun across the wet sand.
A dawn-light pill.

Vertigo

A tiny bit of bone broke off
into my middle ear
& made the world spin
a tiny glacier calved
into my brain's dark sea
the doctor says this happens to people
the brain's oceans rise
& bits of calcium glacier
knock us off balance
make us forget what we're saying
not as extreme as that photo
of the polar bear bobbing alone
on that melting glacier on that mailer you get
that asks you to help stop the planet
from heating up
this drought
this heat wave today
rising up around us
and this coastline silently disappearing
like the hard edges of my equilibrium pill
dissolving in this glass of water
the doctor says rock your head
back & forth hard & fast
as if you were listening to speed metal
the bone glaciers sometimes shake
back into place
shake this world back into place
my son wailed last night
as I lifted him into bed
he was beyond tired
that point when simple things
fractal in the brain
you put too much pressure
on my feelings he said
& his big sister said when she

was a lot younger like two years ago
she thought feelings were arms too
& that you only got dizzy
when you swung your feelings around
too fast like Pooh just did
looking for the Heffalump
& then she asked what that truck driver
was doing today with his feelings & brain
glaciers before his big rig filigreed the freeway
with 43,208 gallons of wildflower honey.

Aubade

My girls are asleep in the house—Siena
burped and wiped and back down,
Cristina cozied in my indentation
in the bed, happy to have another
hour or two of sleep. I should
be on that path out to my office
but I'm done with the world
of should. I'm walking over the sand hill
toward the shore. The only thing
that separates me from the blackened
reef are two snowy egrets. My foot
disappears into the black salt water, then
my hips, my hands. The water,
that stingray cold. My body doesn't trust
what I tell it to do—it's easier to love
this world than it is to disappear.

Old School

I'm told there'll be a crowd where
I'm supposed to go & I'm grateful
for that—I've gotten a little bit better
at smiling & keeping my skeletons in
but it's still weird being mass-produced.
Separate your art from your money,
Eric D. said before he taught himself
to play his clarinet like a bird. In The Big Book
of Good Advice & Good Intention, no one
says anything about playing your clarinet
like a bird. A brown towhee brings
a stick into the chaparral—such a responsible
bird. Brown makes blue more blue
& so my suit blazer blazes through
this Manzanita dusk. Benjamin
Franklin used to have a big meal
about now, sleep four hours, wake
& read, naked, in front of a fire
for a few more before a second
sleep. Couples made love then, in
between sleeps, never at the end
of a tired day. In The Big Book
of Abnormalities, two sleeps qualify
one for meds. The red ants under
the streetlamp know no rest. The
moon matches the lights in the lobby
& my tie—I don't have the drugs
to sort this out. My electric taxi
is arriving. Stupid Edison.

"Everything I Have Is on the Table, Everything I Love Is out to Sea"

Fragmentary sleep and now
fragmentary body. I'm searching
the internet world for a sense
of self—here, an article on the purple
orchidy flowers that bloom on pennies
and here a video of women
protesting for the right to walk
bare-chested like men. My social
network has new news! But it's
the same as the old news—
birthday wishes, photos of mint leaves
on gold puddings, a million
tiny carpe diems and defeats,
lines at the raw food place, too little
curry in the vindaloo, construction
and a bottleneck on the California
Incline. Another someone wants
more attention from their spouse—
I'm not in this habit of spilling my guts
without great care. Even when
I'm alone in a room I don't want
to be the center of attention. You
didn't notice me at the farmer's market
because the potatoes were so fresh
and I was okay with that. The news
in the food court said they caught
the terrorist because so many people
were taking pictures of themselves
that he couldn't stay in the background
for long. He said, "These days even the moon
is a lens. No one can just gracefully
be alone in a room." A ring of water
on my desk. I hold my mug up in the sky—
daylight moon with a slight chance of rain.
You took off early. Now our daughter

cartwheels her purple leotard
over a blue mat somewhere. Try-
outs. The next time we're alone
together and you're still lonely,
remember, I never promised
to light up a room. More news
on the data feed. A bear has ambled
into a suburban yard. A bather flops
off a turtle floaty, runs into the house.
More hysterics broadcast as a type
of wonder—I am doing what I can
to not become the stranger in this
marriage. Yesterday you were telling me
why the leaves on the bird of paradise
are always torn—I *was* listening.
It dapple shades the new love seat
now. Thank you for letting me
lose my mind for a while.

Acknowledgements

Grateful acknowledgement is made to the editors of the following magazines in which these poems first appeared. Their generosity often surprises me.

Barrow Street: "El Niño, El Viejo, El Viento"
BODY: "God's Work"
The Chattahoochee Review: "Moonlight Sonata for the Oughts"
The Cincinnati Review: "Tidepools"
The Enchanted Verses Literary Review: "Prince Lightening, Prince Thunder"
The Harvard Review: "Androids Don't Just Dream of Electric Sheep" and "Temple"
Jung Journal: Culture & Psyche: "Fable"
Muse A: "Fracture & Want"
Poetry Northwest: "Vertigo"
The Southern Review: "After Party," "Coming-of-Age-Story #∞ / Angry Bastard Theory"
The Southampton Review: "The Snowglobe of My Youth"
Zyzzyva: "Everything I Have Is on the Table, Everything I Love Is out to Sea"

For musical accompaniment: the National, Chicano Batman, LCD Soundsystem, Beethoven's Late Quartets, Thievery Corporation, Gillian Welch, Emily Wells, the Selecter, Linton Kwesi Johnson, MURS, A Tribe Called Quest, Alexander, Dan Auerbach, Louis Jordan, Bob Marley, King Sunny Adé, Tinariwen, Sonic Youth, Fats Waller, Nina Simone, Spain, Coltraine, Miles, Monk, Mingus Mingus Mingus, Arcade Fire, Koop, Sun Ra, Air, Aloe Blacc, the Avengers, Minutemen, Bajofondo, Band of Skulls, the English Beat, Bebel Gilberto, Beck, Billy Bragg, Big Daddy Kane, Neil Young, Bruno Mars, Buzzcocks, EL VY, Chet Baker, David Rawlings, Cornershop, Emilíana Torrini, Erik Satie, Bach's Goldberg Variations, Fatboy Slim, Stiff Little Fingers, the Germs, Fleet Foxes, Feist, Fink, Fugazi, Freakwater, Florence & the Machine, Groove Armada, Hanni El

Khatib, the Human League, Ibrahim Ferrer, Iron & Wine, Iggy Pop, the Ramones, Jack White, Jake Bugg, Jenny Lewis, Jill Scott, Leonard Cohen, Lily Allen, Los Paraguayos, Lucinda Williams, M. Ward, M.I.A., Manu Chao, Maroon 5, Mayer Hawthorne, Mazzy Star, Mercedes Sosa, the Monkey Wrench, Morcheeba, Mudhoney, Nas, Nick Cave & The Bad Seeds, Norah Jones, Nouvelle Vague, Otis Redding, Parliament, Pavement, Pink Martini, Phantogram, Poolside, Portishead, Dead Kennedys, Raphael Saadiq, Barry White, Sade, Sidestepper, Scratch Acid, the Jesus Lizard, Silver Jews, Silversun Pickups, Solomon Burke, the Strokes, Taj Mahal, Talking Heads, Thom Yorke, Ugly Casanova, the Velvet Underground, Violent Femmes, Rough Magic, the White Stripes, Wilco, Wreckless Eric, Wyclef Jean, Willy Mason, The Walking Who, X, X-Ray Spex, Yacht, Yeah Yeah Yeahs, Yma Sumac, Zero 7, Ozo Matli, Denge Fever, Prince, James Brown, and many many more! J

I'm also indebted, always, to my friends, poetry world and other. Thank you to Peter Elliot, Elena Karina Byrne, Major Jackson, Kathryn Nuerenber, Ralph Angel, Marissa Hewatt, Garrett Hongo, Christopher Merrill, Wayne Slappy, Karen Kevorkian, Gail Wronsky, Daneil Tiffany, David Roderick, Daniel Mahoney, Forrest Hammer, and Molly Bendall.

Thank you to my dearest poetry brothers who gave this manuscript careful first reads and suggestions: Marty Williams and Kevin Prufer. This would be a lonely place without you.

Thank you to my father, Joseph Blaustein, who taught me, as he has thousands of others, to see. I often marvel at your generosity. May the planet give you another 94 years!

It is hard to imagine a kinder, more generous, supportive heart on this planet, even after twenty years, than Cristina Amaya.

Liner Notes

"Trigger Warning:": Around the time this was written there were several articles in the paper about students protesting to have classes that might illicit a strong emotional response come with "trigger warnings" on the syllabi.

California Dreaming was written as a sort private jam session to El Vy's first album *Runaway Bunny.*

"Coming-of-Age Story #∞: Angry Bastard Theory": Crazy Bastard Theory is a theory by UCLA professor Daniel M. T. Fessler (funded, in part, by the Pentagon) about how men size each other up, choose sides, and decide to fight.

"What's Going On?": This poem is dedicated to the victims and fellow parents who lived through those tense hours of the 2013 mass shooting in Santa Monica.

"Lemons": The poem's ending is a riff on Li Young Li's "Persimmons."

"Androids Don't Just Dream of Electric Sheep": The title is a silly answer to Phillip K. Dick's "Do Androids Dream of Electric Sheep?" He always said he was terrible at titles but, as a teenager, I loved his anthropomorphic question.

"Old School": Wikipedia (!) states that Thomas Edison "was one of the first inventors to apply the principles of mass production and large-scale teamwork to the process of invention." Of course there was the printing press, but if Wikipedia said it, it must be true.

"Everything I Have Is on the Table, Everything I Love Is out to Sea":
The title is borrowed from the National's "Don't Swallow the Cap"
from the album *Trouble Will Find Me*. Other lines and narratives in
this book riff on that album. The title is used here with permission of
the National.